MILITARY MACHINES

SPY PLANES

By Therese Shea

Gareth Stevens
Publishing

Please visit our website, www.garethstevens.com. For a free color catalog of all our high-quality books, call toll free 1-800-542-2595 or fax 1-877-542-2596.

Library of Congress Cataloging-in-Publication Data

Shea, Therese.
 Spy planes / Therese Shea.
    p. cm. — (Military machines)
 Includes index.
 ISBN 978-1-4339-8473-0 (pbk.)
 ISBN 978-1-4339-8474-7 (6-pack)
 ISBN 978-1-4339-8472-3 (library binding)
 1. Reconnaissance aircraft. I. Title.
 UG1242.R4S54 2012
 358.4'5830973—dc23
                                            2012031289

First Edition

Published in 2013 by
Gareth Stevens Publishing
111 East 14th Street, Suite 349
New York, NY 10003

Copyright © 2013 Gareth Stevens Publishing

Designer: Michael J. Flynn
Editor: Kristen Rajczak

Photo credits: Cover, pp. 1, 10–11, 20 Erik Simonsen/Photographer's Choice/Getty Images; courtesy of the US Air Force: pp. 4, 13 by Senior Airman Levi Riendeau, 14–15, 18–19, 24 by Staff Sgt. Rhiannon Willard, 28–29 by Senior Airman Tiffany Trojca, 29 by Staff Sgt. Manuel J. Martinez; pp. 5, 11 USAF/Getty Images; p. 7 Buyenlarge/Archive Photos/Getty Images; courtesy of the US Navy: pp. 8, 26–27; p. 9 Patrick Aventurier/ Gamma-Rapho/Getty Images; p. 12 Keystone/Hulton Archive/Getty Images; p. 17 STR/AFP/Getty Images; p. 21 NASA/Getty Images; pp. 22–23 Stocktrek Images/Getty Images; pp. 25, 27 US Navy/Getty Images.

Printed in the United States of America

CPSIA compliance information: Batch #CW13GS: For further information contact Gareth Stevens, New York, New York at 1-800-542-2595.

CONTENTS

Words in the glossary appear in **bold** type the first time they are used in the text.

REAL-LIFE SPIES

You've probably seen movies about spies collecting valuable **information** for their country. They may have incredibly cool gadgets and ways of getting around. But that's just the movies, right? Yes and no. There *are* real-life spies, and they do use some really cool **technology**.

Spy planes have been one of the best ways for many governments to gather information over the past few decades. You probably won't hear the word "spy" used much, though. "Reconnaissance" and "surveillance" are more common terms to describe these planes and their activities. Both simply mean gathering information about countries' secret activities, which is called intelligence.

The US military collects information about other countries during times of war and peace.

Reconnaissance and Surveillance

The meanings of "reconnaissance" and "surveillance" are similar, but the terms are used differently in the military. Surveillance aids in a short-term mission. For example, a crew in a spy plane might communicate intelligence that would result in soldiers calling off an attack because the enemy's forces are too large. Reconnaissance missions are usually for long-term intelligence-gathering purposes.

THE FIRST SPY AIRCRAFT

The beginning of air reconnaissance wasn't in planes but in hot-air balloons! During the American Civil War, the Union Army had a balloon force. Thaddeus Lowe was the "aeronaut" who helped convince President Abraham Lincoln to use hot-air balloons to view enemy positions from a distance. Lowe even sent telegrams of what he saw from up in the balloon!

Hot-air balloons were used in World War I, too. By this time, fighter planes had taken to the air, so balloons became a target. To fight back, some balloons were loaded with explosives. An attacking plane could be badly **damaged** after trying to take down one of these balloons.

Drones

Drones are planes that have been in the news a lot recently. They're used to gather information, much like reconnaissance planes. However, drones don't have a pilot on board. Instead, people on the ground or in another plane control the drone using computers and technology somewhat like a video game system.

Led by Lowe, the balloon force would make thousands of reconnaissance flights during the Civil War.

THE U-2

After World War II, the United States and the Soviet Union weren't on friendly terms. This was the start of the Cold War, a time period when these nations worried about each other's military activity. They built up stores of weapons and **vehicles** in case an actual war broke out.

The Lockheed Corporation built the first U-2 airplane in 1954 under the order of President Dwight Eisenhower. He wanted a high-flying reconnaissance aircraft for the purpose of collecting intelligence about the Soviet Union. The U-2 could reach heights of 70,000 feet (21,336 m) and stay in the air for more than 8 hours at a time.

The U-2 only required one pilot.

The U-2 spy plane has been used for many years. This picture was taken in 1996.

The Dragon Lady

The U-2 was nicknamed the Dragon Lady after a comic strip character. However, pilots say that flying one is like flying a wild beast. The U-2 is light so it can fly high, but rough patches of air can cause a pilot to lose control. Landing is challenging because it doesn't have normal landing gear, which is very heavy.

The U-2 was ready to be tested by 1956. Because of its light body, it required a skilled pilot. The air force chose Hervey Stockman, an airman who had flown 68 **combat** missions during World War II.

On July 4, 1956, Stockman flew a U-2 from West Germany into the Soviet Union. He flew over shipyards and military bases. His plane was spotted by Soviet **radar**, however. MiG fighters were sent to **intercept** it, but the plane was just too high for the Soviet jets. Stockman safely landed back in West Germany 8 hours and 45 minutes after he had left.

During Hervey Stockman's flight, the winds at the U-2's height, or altitude, were so strong that they crushed the fuel tank.

Dangerous Mission

Hervey Stockman's mission was a dangerous one. He had nothing on him to identify him as a US airman. He wouldn't have had any protection if enemies had captured him. According to his nephew, he also had a poisonous pill with him. He was ordered to eat it to avoid being captured.

Francis Gary Powers

In 1960, air force pilot Francis Gary Powers was shot down in a U-2 by a Soviet surface-to-air **missile** (SAM). It's thought that Soviet spies had found out about the flight beforehand. Powers parachuted from the plane and landed safely in the Soviet Union. He was held prisoner for nearly 2 years before he was released.

This event proved that other countries' new aircraft and defense systems had made the U-2 a less valuable reconnaissance tool. The military began to look for other planes. However, the U-2 continues to be used today for many purposes. Though newer spy planes have since been retired, there's no sign yet that the U-2 will be.

Cuban Missile Crisis

In 1962, President John F. Kennedy asked for proof that the Soviets were supplying Cuba with missiles. The CIA (Central Intelligence Agency) gave him photos taken from a U-2 at 72,000 feet (21,946 m). It showed medium-range missiles that could reach the United States. This sparked the Cuban Missile Crisis.

Today's U-2, the U-2S, has updated engines and new cameras and sensors. Since 2003, the air force has flown more than 95,000 hours in its 33 U-2s.

THE A-12

With the **development** of SAMs, the military knew another reconnaissance plane was needed. The A-12 could fly higher than the U-2 and was four times faster. The onboard photo technology provided sharper, clearer images, too. However, by the time Lockheed's A-12 was ready in the early 1960s, Soviet radar systems were able to locate it and similar aircraft in their skies.

The development of the A-12 was called Project Oxcart.

U.S. AIR FORCE

The A-12s were still valuable, however, and ran many missions in Asia. The first mission, in 1967, was over North Vietnam. The resulting photos revealed 70 SAM sites. The A-12 flew 29 more missions over Asia, but was retired in May 1968.

UFOs Identified?

Area 51 is an air force base in Nevada. Over the years, the air force, the CIA, and Lockheed have tested aircraft there, including the U-2 and the A-12. Most Area 51 operations are extremely secretive. Is it any wonder UFOs (Unidentified Flying Objects) have often been reported near the base?

In 1968, North Koreans captured the US naval ship *Pueblo*, which had been traveling through nearby waters. The US government didn't know where the ship and its crew were being held. They also didn't know if North Korea was building up weapons to start a war. Some American officials suggested bombing parts of North Korea.

However, the government decided to collect intelligence instead. An A-12 flew over North Korea and found the exact location of the *Pueblo*. There were no signs the North Koreans were preparing for war. The American government used this information to peacefully **negotiate** for the release of the crew.

Satellite Photoreconnaissance

By the 1960s, the United States was using **satellites** to collect intelligence. From 1960 to 1972, a satellite project called Corona took more than 800,000 photos of many areas of the Soviet Union. However, it took time for the film to return so the photos could be reviewed. Spy planes were needed to provide information in a shorter period of time.

The USS *Pueblo* remains in North Korea as a museum ship today.

THE SR-71

From 1966 to 1990, the SR-71 was the air force's—and the world's—highest-flying and fastest-moving aircraft. On July 28, 1976, it set two world records for a plane of its kind—achieving an average speed of 2,193.167 miles (3,528.81 km) per hour and an altitude of 85,068.997 feet (25,929.08 m). Unlike the A-12, the SR-71 had side-facing cameras and radar. This meant it didn't have to fly over enemy territory in order to gather intelligence. It could safely stay over friendly nations.

The SR-71, nicknamed the Blackbird, had a crew of two: a pilot and a reconnaissance systems officer. Because of the altitude, they wore suits similar to those worn by astronauts.

Taking Off in a Blackbird

The SR-71 had to take off with very little fuel in its tanks. It was then refueled in the air. When its six fuel tanks were filled, it could fly 2,500 miles (4,023 km). At rest on the ground, fuel leaked out constantly since the tanks only sealed at operating temperatures.

Each SR-71 cost
about $34 million.

SR-71s saw action through several decades. In 1972, they accompanied B-52s as they dropped bombs over North Vietnam. They took surveillance photos to locate SAM sites that shot back at the B-52s. In 1987, SR-71s flew a number of missions over the Persian Gulf, revealing Iranian missile sites.

The SR-71 was retired in 1990 due in part to its high cost. However, in 1994, Congress reactivated three for missions best suited to only the SR-71. Of the 32 built, none was ever lost to enemy fire, despite the fact that they were shot at more than 1,000 times over 26 years.

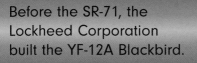
Before the SR-71, the Lockheed Corporation built the YF-12A Blackbird.

The last SR-71
mission was flown
in 1999.

The Skunk Works

The Skunk Works was the name for a special division
of Lockheed. In its most famous days, it was headed by
engineer Clarence "Kelly" Johnson. Johnson and his team
began working with the US military in 1943, building an
XP-80 jet fighter in just 143 days. However, the SR-71 was
probably their most famous creation.

THE RC-135

The RC-135 is a reconnaissance plane built by the Boeing Company for the US Air Force. The large plane can carry up to 27 crewmembers, and it's loaded with electronic surveillance equipment. Onboard sensors collect data and send communications to base using satellites. To date, 32 RC-135s have been built since 1964. There are 14 kinds, each with different equipment for different situations.

The RC-135 is based at Offutt Air Force Base in Nebraska.

Originally used for intelligence only, the RC-135 was later transferred to Air Combat Command. Since then, RC-135s have participated in every major US armed conflict including Vietnam, Grenada, Panama, Iraq, and Afghanistan.

RC-135s in Afghanistan

RC-135s proved useful in the war in Afghanistan. They can intercept communications and pass on intelligence to troops on the ground. This information helped save civilian lives and pinpoint enemies. More than 7,000 missions using the RC-135 and other spy planes were flown in a single year during this war.

THE EP-3E ARIES II

The EP-3E ARIES II is a reconnaissance plane for the US Navy. ARIES stands for Airborne Reconnaissance Integrated Electronic System. The first EP-3Es were built in the 1960s and 1970s. The ARIES II was developed in the late 1990s.

This plane can have a crew of 22 or more, including three pilots. It has five fuel tanks, four engines, and can fly for 12 hours or around 3,450 miles (5,551 km). Its maximum speed is 466 miles (750 km) per hour. Its sensors, receivers, and **antennae** pick up and record telephone calls, e-mails, faxes, and satellite transmissions. This EP-3E has no weapons to attack others or protect itself.

The EP-3E has an object attached under the plane called a radome. It keeps the radar antennae safe.

The EP-3E has been a reliable reconnaissance plane for the US military.

Born from the P-3C

The P3 has been a US Navy aircraft since the 1960s. The P-3C Orion is an antisubmarine and antisurface warfare plane as well as a reconnaissance plane—which means it carries weapons, including missiles and torpedoes. In the 1990s, some P-3Cs became EP-3E ARIES IIs.

The EP-3E's crew used an ax and hot coffee to try to damage the plane's equipment so the Chinese couldn't learn too much about US technology and intelligence.

In 2001, a Chinese fighter jet crashed into an EP-3E ARIES II over the South China Sea. The Chinese pilot was killed in the crash, and the EP-3E made an emergency landing at a Chinese airbase. The Chinese and US governments disagreed about the details of the crash. The US crew denied being in Chinese airspace at the time. They also claimed the Chinese jets were flying dangerously close to them and caused the crash.

The Chinese held the American crew of 24 for 2 weeks. They kept the plane—and all its valuable equipment—for several more months before it was returned.

Recce Pilots, Quiet Heroes

Reconnaissance, or recce (REH-kee), pilots rarely get their names in newspapers. Their risky missions are secret. If all goes well, no one outside of their organization knows about them. Sadly, since the 1950s, more than 170 airmen have lost their lives on reconnaissance missions.

In order to bring the damaged EP-3E back to the United States, it had to be taken apart!

THE SKIES OF TOMORROW

Countries such as China have asked that the United States cease flying planes near their borders. The United States, in turn, asks that these nations be more open about their military operations. Until countries can trust each other, there will be a need to keep an eye on one another from the skies.

An air force spokesman called the MC-12W a "flying intelligence shop." It has the added bonus of being able to fly through bad weather, unlike drones.

Though the US drone program is expanding, drone bombing programs have been the cause of the deaths of ordinary citizens in enemy territory. The military may need to use manned planes in addition to drones to better fight the enemy in the future. The skills and knowledge of human pilots in spy planes can't be replaced.

The advanced technology in the cockpit of the MC-12W helps pilots fly safely while completing dangerous missions.

The MC-12W

The MC-12W Liberty is a four-crew plane much like many civilian aircraft. The newest of the air force spy planes, it has brought in intelligence—such as the location of roadside bombs in Iraq and Afghanistan—that continues to save lives. Onboard video can be transmitted to soldiers on the ground.

GLOSSARY

antenna: a metal rod or wire used to send and receive radio waves

combat: armed fighting between opposing forces

damage: harm. Also, to cause harm.

development: the act or process of creating over time

information: knowledge obtained from study or observation

intercept: to stop or interrupt the course or delivery of something

missile: a rocket used to strike something at a distance

mission: a task or job a group must perform

negotiate: to come to an agreement

radar: a machine that uses radio waves to locate and identify objects

satellite: an object that circles Earth

technology: the practical application of specialized knowledge

vehicle: an object used for carrying or transporting people or goods, such as a car, truck, or airplane

FOR MORE INFORMATION

Books

Braulick, Carrie A. *U.S. Air Force Spy Planes.* Mankato, MN: Capstone Press, 2007.

David, Jack. *U-2 Planes.* Minneapolis, MN: Bellwether Media, 2008.

Graham, Richard. *Flying the SR-71 Blackbird: In the Cockpit on a Secret Operational Mission.* St. Paul, MN: Zenith Press, 2008.

Websites

How a U.S. Spy Plane Works
www.howstuffworks.com/spy-plane.htm
Read more about the EP-3E, and see photos of it in flight.

SR-71 Revealed! Operational Sortie
www.habus.org/revealed/sortie.htm
See what it takes to fly a SR-71, from starting the engine to landing.

U-2 High-Altitude Reconnaissance Aircraft
www.airforce-technology.com/projects/u2/
Learn about the U-2, a US spy plane since 1955.

INDEX